Meghan's World

The Story of One Girl's Triumph over Sensory Processing Disorder

Written by DIANE M. RENNA
Illustrated by REGINA STARK
With Illustrations by MEGHAN RENNA

Indigo Impressions
Speonk, New York

Published by Indigo Impressions
P.O. Box 501
Speonk, NY 11972-0501

Publisher's Cataloging-in-Publication Data
Renna, Diane M.

Meghan's World : The Story of One Girl's Triumph over Sensory Processing Disorder / Diane M. Renna. – Speonk, NY : Indigo Impressions, 2007.

p. ; cm.
ISBN: 0-9788339-0-2
ISBN13: 978-0-9788339-0-9

1. Sensory integration dysfunction in children. 2. Sensory disorders--Treatment. I. Title.

RJ506.S44 R46 2006
616.85/82—dc22 2   2006932615

Project coordination by Jenkins Group, Inc • www.BookPublishing.com
Book design and layout by Eric Tufford

Printed in Singapore
11 10 09 08 07 • 5 4 3 2 1

For more information about Regina Stark and to view/purchase her other works of art, please visit
www.centerforartandhealing.com

Disclaimer: The ideas/therapies presented in this book are based on sensory processing and behavior. The reader is cautioned that not all suggestions are appropriate to all individuals, and consultation with a professional is recommended. Neither the author nor the publisher imply any direct or indirect endorsement of a specific recommendation or activity for an individual person.

www.meghanstriumphoverspd.com

✱ A Brief Explanation ✱

"The theory and treatment of sensory integration was developed by Dr. A. Jean Ayres, OTR, in the 1960s in an attempt to understand and explain some of the connections between learning and the functioning of the nervous system. She developed specific testing and treatment to provide what she felt was the optimal treatment for learning disabled children who had sensory processing problems. Not all children with learning disabilities have sensory integrative dysfunction, but sensory integrative dysfunction often has an impact on learning and behavior.

Sensory Integration is a normal process by which the sensory systems provide information about our bodies and the world around us. The brain and the rest of the nervous system take that information and organize it so that we can learn, move, and behave normally. This is sensory processing, or sensory integration. All people process sensory information, some more efficiently than others...

When the normal process of sensory integration is not efficient, we label it **sensory integration dysfunction**. This simply means that parts of this processing system are not providing information reliably. Sensory Integration Dysfunction (often labeled DSI) can interfere with an individual's ability to attend, develop motor skills, regulate behavior and organize tasks, complete self-care skills (for example, dressing and eating), develop visual and auditory skills, and to feel comfortable in the environment."

Above quote from *Including SI for Parents* by Jeanne Sangirardi Ganz, OTR/L BCP

Please note that Sensory Processing Dysfunction (SPD) has many names/labels, including Sensory Integration Dysfunction and Dysfunctional Sensory Integration.

* A Note from the Author *

Meghan's World was written to validate the feelings of children suffering with Sensory Processing Disorder (SPD) and other disabilities/delays that often go side-by-side with SPD. I wanted the children and their parents to know that they are not alone, and that there are resources available to make their lives less stressful, more comfortable, and happy. Living with SPD can be a challenge, but there are therapies and strategies that can help make their world a better place.

Meghan's World briefly describes our experiences with SPD and what has helped us. You may not need every therapy, and each may affect you differently. If you are considering a therapy, I recommend that you do the research beforehand, ask other parents/therapists about their experiences, and then seek the advice of a professional who specializes in that particular therapy. In the back of *Meghan's World*, there is a "Therapies and Helpful Information" section where you can find more information about what is available to help your child. Also note that SPD comes with many gifts—I encourage you to foster your children's gifts and to let them express themselves and be all they can be.

Because of SPD, we have learned and grown together as a family. We have learned to appreciate the simple things in life. We wish you all the success that we have seen in our journey, and great memories to last a lifetime.

Diane M. Renna

To Meghan, Michael, Gavin, Lorenzo ... Love you lots.

To all children and families dealing with SPD ...
You will see the rainbow.

Thank you to everyone who has supported
and helped me with this book!

DMR

To my sons, Robert and Eddie,
for all the love and support
I receive from you always.

To my father, the late Robert W. Gillies,
whose spirit lives on in all the work I do.

RS

Meghan was sad as she dressed for her spring concert. She wanted to wear her new dress, but the fabric was scratchy and the sleeves were tight. Meghan couldn't understand why she felt uncomfortable in clothes that she really wanted to wear. She started to cry. It always took a long time to find an outfit. She called Mom for help.

Mom noticed Meghan was upset.
She gave her a long hug and a kiss.
Eventually, they found a dress and a
comfortable pair of shoes.

Meghan didn't like the way her hair felt on her
face. It always bothered her, so Mom gently pulled
it back. Mom used a wooden brush that had soft, firm
nylon bristles. It was the only brush that felt okay.
This cheered Meghan up.
Now she was ready for
her big night.
She looked beautiful.

Time passed. Mom, Dad, Meghan and her brother, Michael, were finishing dinner. Meghan was a picky eater and often ate cold broccoli and pasta. It was hard for her to feel when she was full. So, Mom told Meghan to eat three pieces of broccoli and two more bites of pasta until her plate looked almost empty.

Mom and Dad were happy and couldn't wait to see Meghan perform. Her class had been practicing all week and they were ready for the spring concert. Meghan's class was excited about their moving-up ceremony, and they were eager to sing the new songs they had learned.

The teachers were proud because the kids had worked hard all year. Grandma and Grandpa were meeting them at the school. Everyone couldn't wait for the show to begin.

Once Meghan reached the classroom, she began to feel uneasy. It was noisy. She could hear the cars driving by outside.

The girls were talking loudly. The boys were running around. She was afraid someone might bump into her.

Sure enough, Peter ran by yelling and bumped into her arm. It stung, so she rubbed it. Her ears hurt, so she covered them with her hands. Soon after, Meghan sat at a table away from the other kids and put her head down for a break. It was almost time for the show to start.

Suddenly, Miss Patty entered the room and asked the students to form a line. Meghan could hear the music and Miss Theresa greeting the audience in the auditorium. Meghan's heart began to pound really fast. Her arm felt a little better, but her ears still hurt. She tried not to think about it.

The show was starting. Meghan worried that someone might bump into her again. She decided to walk slowly. She cuddled herself as she entered and sat down on stage.

Meghan's chair was cold and hard, and it hurt her bottom. The sight of all the people in the audience made her feel anxious. The noise in the room echoed. The lights were bright. Meghan tried to sing, but she was scared. She had a headache and her tummy felt funny. Her ears began to hurt even more. Meghan couldn't stand the sound of the audience clapping and laughing.

Miss Theresa called Meghan's name to receive her certificate. She was nervous, but happy. Mom took pictures and Dad videotaped as she shyly accepted her scroll.

Grandma and Grandpa beamed with pride.

Meghan was their first grandchild.

By the time the tenth student received her certificate, Meghan couldn't take the sound of the clapping and all the other noises: the cars outside, the music, the talking, and their echoes.

She began to press her hands together, pull her dress, hit herself, and cover her ears. Eventually, she stood up and yelled, "STOP!"

Meghan felt like she was falling apart. However, she couldn't leave her seat until the end of the show. Meghan felt miserable and needed a hug.

When the show was over, Meghan went down and hugged her mom. Then she got a drink and a cupcake. The students had prepared desserts for their guests and everyone was enjoying them.

Meghan felt relieved that the show was over. She was ready to go home. She was exhausted and fell asleep in the car.

When they got home, Mom tucked Meghan into bed. Afterward, Mom went downstairs to watch the video with Dad. Mom and Dad were sad that Meghan felt uncomfortable and did not enjoy her first school show.

They wanted her to feel safe and happy in the outside world, just as she did at home.

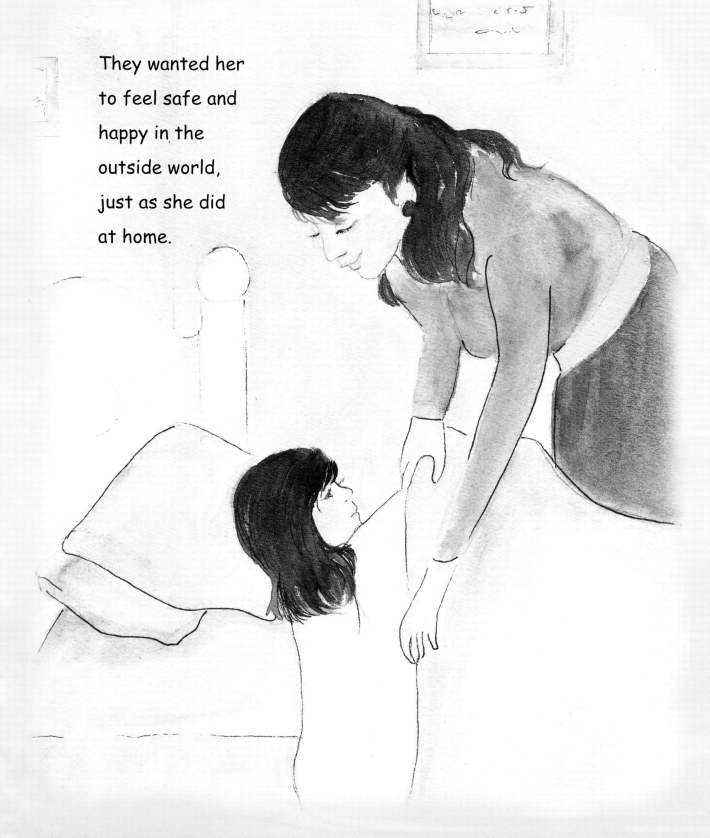

Soon after, Mom read a report written by an occupational therapist (OT), Miss Jeanne, about Sensory Processing Disorder (SPD). The more Mom read, the more it described Meghan's sensitivities to sight, sound, touch, smell, and movement. It was then that Mom made the call to have Miss Jeanne evaluate Meghan. Miss Jeanne specialized in SPD.

Meghan had fun at the evaluation. Miss Jeanne was pretty, funny, and had a cool OT room. Meghan played with the squishy balls, trampoline, balance beam, ball pit, and swings while Mom filled out paperwork. Mom was happy to see Meghan enjoying herself.

Meghan and Mom were glad to meet Miss Jeanne.
She helped everything make sense. Miss Jeanne made up a plan
called a "sensory diet" to help Meghan feel more comfortable.

The sensory diet provided the sensory activities Meghan needed to address her sensory preferences and her sensory sensitivities. Meghan played fun games, did challenging obstacle courses, and did gymnastic-type exercises to work her muscles.

In the fall, Meghan started a new school. The new school was not as noisy, the lights were not as bright, and she felt more comfortable there. In no time, she made two friends, Jenna and Natalie. They loved to play together.

At the new school, Meghan went to OT classes twice a week. She swung on swings, played with scooters, and did other fun stuff. She felt better after going to OT class.

Meghan's school OT, Miss Laura, told Mom about some therapies that would help Meghan.

First, Miss Laura taught Mom the Brushing Protocol.*

Mom had to brush Meghan with a special brush often. This helped
Meghan feel calmer. She was able to sit and eat at the dinner table.
She watched TV without having to get up and move around.
She could play without worrying about anyone bumping into her.
Meghan felt happier after being brushed. It was like a massage.

*See Therapies and Helpful Information section—Wilbarger Brushing Protocol

Another therapy was called Therapeutic Listening.®
Meghan listened, at home, to special music through headphones for
six weeks, twice a day for thirty minutes. Miss Laura oversaw the
program. This helped Meghan's ears feel better. She felt happy, calm,
and organized. She was able to look people in the eye and enjoy
conversations with her friends and adults. Meghan even slept better.

However, since Meghan was extremely sensitive to sound, Mom decided to bring Meghan to a therapist who specialized in auditory therapy* to retrain her hearing. This helped Meghan's tactile (touch) issues and modulation (sensory processing).

Meghan listened to special music, twice a day, for thirty minutes. She did this for ten days in a row at the therapist's office. Mom also had sound sensitivity, so she did the therapy with Meghan. They had fun. They did puzzles, played with scented dough, colored, and drew while they listened. The auditory therapy* pinpointed the exact frequencies that were bothering them. Afterward, they were able to hear more clearly, and noises didn't hurt their ears anymore.

*See Therapies and Helpful Information section—Berard Auditory Intervention Therapy

Meghan also saw a child psychologist a few times.

They played together and Meghan learned how to socially express herself better.
The world seemed less scary after playing with Miss Cynthia.

Eventually, Meghan went to an allergy doctor.

She had several earaches and was sick often. She developed allergy-induced asthma. The allergy doctor found out she was allergic to milk, wheat, and some other foods. She went on a special diet and started feeling a little better.

The next step was seeing a nutritionist monthly for over a year. Meghan had to take some special supplements to heal her tummy and make her strong.

Mom mixed the supplements in pineapple juice or cinnamon apple sauce to make them taste good.

Meghan also started taking baths in Epsom salts. They made her feel calm and relaxed. She had fun playing in the tub.

Good news came when Mom learned about digestive enzymes from another mom on an SPD online support group. The enzymes help Meghan digest foods she is intolerant to.

After starting the enzymes, her tummy started to feel better. She grew taller and gained weight. She became a healthy girl. Meghan was happy. She didn't need the allergy and asthma medicine daily anymore.

The last therapy was vision therapy. Meghan went to a behavioral optometrist. He gave her eye exercises and a computer program to use at home. Meghan did the eye exercises three times a week for fifteen minutes. She did this for over a year. The doctor also made special bifocal glasses for her. Now she can read better and see the blackboard more clearly at school.

In addition to the therapies, Meghan enjoys doing lots of physical activities. They make her feel good. She loves to go to yoga, gymnastics, swimming, and dance classes.

She makes more friends and has tons of fun.

At home, Meghan has an OT room with indoor swings, a trapeze, a mini trampoline, and a cool hideaway in the closet.

She loves to go there to get the wiggles out.

Meghan likes to relax in the hideaway when she needs a break from the outside world. She loves to listen to music and swing on the swing. This helps her to unwind and feel at peace.

Meghan often plays on her play set and trampoline. She rides bikes, roller skates, and makes chalk drawings with her friends, Cassie and Alison. On summer days, she swims in her pool. On winter days, she plays in the snow. Meghan loves to be outside and she enjoys nature. She appreciates all the wonders the Earth has to offer. She is also a great artist who loves to draw and paint.

The therapies Meghan did were a lot of work, but she had fun. Now Meghan can wear stockings, jeans, and the outfit of her choice. She doesn't take long to get dressed. She can go to parades and out to eat. She enjoys singing in school shows. She loves playing with her friends and family.

But most of all, Meghan is happy, healthy, and feels great about herself.

✱ Therapies and Helpful Information ✱

The Wilbarger Brushing Protocol – Should only be initiated by a trained OT. Parents are advised not to start on their own because brushing is very stimulating to the nervous system. Joint compressions follow the brushing and this therapy needs to be directed by a trained professional for safety reasons.

Berard Auditory Integration Training (Berard AIT) – Dr. Guy Berard's official website, which lists trained practitioners: www.drguyberard.com

Society for Auditory Intervention Techniques – Learn about different listening therapies and theories: www.autismwebsite.com/saitwebsite/index.html

Vital Links – The Therapeutic Listening® website is tailored to meet the needs of the individual using electronically altered CDs via a trained sensory integrative professional; lists trained practitioners: www.vitallinks.net

Vision Therapy – Eye exercises and glasses to improve vision for learning/school, provided by a behavioral optometrist: www.optometrists.org

Diana A. Henry MS, OTR/L and Henry OT Services – brings the "ateachabout" program to your community, providing workshops, sensory "tools," information on designing "sensory safe spaces," and the Sensory Processing Measure (SPM) to support parents, therapists, teachers, and students in home and school: **www.ateachabout.com**

www.southpawenterprises.com – develops suspended equipment and "cozy" materials for clinics, schools, and homes for all ages, including early intervention: (800) 228-1698

www.developmentaldelayresources.org – provides a network for parents and professionals and current information after the diagnosis to support children with special needs.

Book by Lucy Jane Miller, Ph.D., OTR – *Sensational Kids: Hope and Help for Children with Sensory Processing Disorder (SPD)*

The Early Intervention Program – Call your local school district to find out how to get an evaluation and services for your child.

Wrights Law Website – Accurate, up-to-date information about special education law and advocacy for children with disabilities: www.wrightslaw.com

SPD Parent Connections – Resources for the SPD community; parent support group, connections and information: www.sinetwork.org

Karen DeFelice's Enzyme Website and Books – *Enzymes for Autism and other Neurological Conditions* includes topics other than enzymes, including Epsom salts baths, vitamins, the digestive system, and special diets: www.enzymestuff.com

Houstonni Enzymes – To purchase enzymes: www.houstonni.com

Yahoo Health Groups: sid-dsi Sensory Integration Disorder Group – Great group for support, understanding, and knowledge; informative files and links section: DIS-Brasil-subscribe@yahoogroups

Books by Carol Stock Kranowitz, M.A. – *The Out of Sync Child, The Out of Sync Child Has Fun, 101 Activities for Kids in Tight Places;* great resources to gain knowledge, understanding, and ideas.

Book by Jeanne Ganz, OTR/L,BCP – *Including SI for Parents - Sensory Integration Strategies for Home and School* is an excellent resource for understanding SPD; gives helpful tips on managing SPD in your child.

www.sensoryresources.com – "Resources for raising children with sensory motor, developmental, and social and emotional challenges."

www.theraproducts.com – A company that sells tons of sensory friendly toys, books, and other useful learning products.

www.theragifts.com – Another site for sensory friendly products.

www.PlayAwayToy.com – Indoor swing and accessories site: (888) 752-9929

Activities – Yoga, gymnastics, horseback riding, karate, dance, and swimming

Lifestyle – Eat natural and organic foods whenever possible for optimum health; SPD kids digest and handle natural foods better than foods with additives, hormones, and dyes.

Alternatives to Consider – Nutritionist, chiropractor, acupuncturist (NAET allergy elimination technique: http://www.naet.com), homeopathy; search the web to learn more about these topics.

* All about Me *

My name is _____

Today's date is _____

I am special.
Here is a picture of me

My favorite foods are _____

My favorite colors are _____

My favorite things to do are _____

_____

What I like about myself is _____

_____

What I would change about myself is _____

_____

I feel sad when _____

_____

I feel happy when _____

_____

I would like to try _____ therapy/ies

to help me feel better with _____

because it bothers me or makes me feel uncomfortable.

I would like to be _____ when I am older.